EU NUCLEAR ENERGY POLICY

Todor A. Shukerov

Todor A. Shukerov holds a LLM International Commercial Law degree from University of Nottingham and a Master of Law degree from University of Plovdiv.

After his graduation from University of Plovdiv Todor completed a traineeship programme at Bulgarian courts. Subsequently, Todor was awarded with an EU Taught Masters Scholarship from University of Nottingham where he was accepted in the LLM International Commercial Law course. During his studies at University of Nottingham Todor specialised in Intellectual Property Law, EU Competition Law and International Sale of Goods. In his dissertation, entitled *"COPYRIGH LAW vs. FILE SHARING IN EUROPE"* and awarded with Distinction, Todor analysed the legal framework in relation to peer-to-peer file sharing technology in Europe.

After the completion of his studies in University of Nottingham Todor provided legal, administrative and commercial support to German investors developing 12-MW photovoltaic (solar) power plant in Bulgaria, a project amounted to nearly EUR 25 millions and successfully finished in the summer of 2012.

In his professional experience in the Council of the EU (at the Industry, Space, Research and Innovation Unit of Directorate General Economic Affairs and Competitiveness) and in the course of negotiations concerning the research and training of the European Atomic Energy Community (2014 - 2018), part of Horizon 2020 programme, Todor carried out in-depth research and analysis of the European Union nuclear energy policy which resulted in this book.

The author alone is responsible for the facts and opinions expressed in this book.

2013

Brussels

EU Nuclear Energy Policy

CONTENTS

EU Nuclear Energy Policy

I. Introduction

Before the nuclear meltdown accident in Fukushima nuclear plant caused by tsunami in 2011, nuclear energy in Europe was considered as an important energy source for the upcoming years. Although not so long time ago the nuclear energy was unconditionally rejected by almost every European decision-maker[1], the debate about its use as an energy source had experienced a significant comeback. However, currently European countries remain largely divided on the role nuclear energy should play in the EU energy market in the forthcoming decades.

In general, the importance of nuclear energy debate stems from three factors: the EU's growing import dependency, the high oil and gas prices, and the limited success of the fight against climate change. Firstly, the EU is heavily depended on foreign energy supply and its import dependency is even expected to rise. It was estimated that in next 25 years around 70 % of EU's energy needs, compared to around 53% in 2010, will be met by imported products.[2] Since not all of Europe's energy partners

---

[1] At the fifth conference of the parties to the UNFCCC (COP-5) in 1999, EU explicitly rejected the idea that nuclear power could help solving the climate change problem. It is worth mentioning that this happened under the presidency of Finland, the first EU Member State to start building a new nuclear power plant a few years later.

[2] EC Green Paper *"A European Strategy for Sustainable, Competitive and Secure Energy"* COM (2006) 105, 8 March 2006, available from *http://ec.europa.eu/energy/green-paper-energy/doc/2006_03_08_gp_document_en.pdf*;
EC *"EU Energy in Figures - Statistical pocketbook 2012"* (2012) available from

have been considered fully reliable, the EU needs to avoid the use of energy supply as a political weapon. Therefore, the potential growth of import dependency increases the EU's need for competitive domestic energy sources, including the use of nuclear energy. Secondly, as the global demand for energy is increasing, oil and gas prices remain high and volatile. It is not likely the issues around gas and oil supply to be solved in the immediate future; hence nuclear power can be used as an alternative to overcome those problems. Thirdly, the EU is very committed to combat climate change, but it is still struggling to attain its Kyoto goals. It is believed that nuclear energy can significantly help the fight against global warming and climate change as it contributes to the reduction of greenhouse gas emissions. Nowadays, nuclear energy contributes to around 30 % of the EU's electricity generation, which represents two-thirds of its carbon-free electricity production, and provides a constant base-load electricity supply, thereby reducing dependence on fossil fuels.[3]

It can be said that the nuclear energy is per definition a matter of European interest. The Chernobyl nuclear disaster in 1986 affected almost the whole continent and showed that the health and safety risks of nuclear power do not stop at national borders. Furthermore, decisions taken by one Member State relating to nuclear energy have immediate consequences on other Member

---

http://ec.europa.eu/energy/publications/doc/2012_energy_figures.pdf

[3] EC, DG Research and Innovation "Euratom FP7 Research & Training Projects" (2012), Volume 3, EUR 24859 EN, p. 7.

States in terms of oil and gas dependency, carbon dioxide emissions, environmental protection and competitiveness.

The aim of this paper is to analyse the EU's policy in addressing the use of nuclear energy. In next chapter, the debate around nuclear power will be discussed followed by an overview on the current status of nuclear energy in the EU and its Member States. In the fourth chapter, the EU policy instruments in the field nuclear power will be examined together with the EU's position towards main nuclear issues. Then, the paper will scrutinise the problems accompanying the application of nuclear safety rules by the Member States. The sixth chapter will take a look at the nuclear research carried out under the current Framework Programme, as well as at the EU participation in certain international research projects. And finally the discussion will focus on the prospects of nuclear energy in Europe.

II. Nuclear Debate

Generally, the debate around nuclear energy is characterised by a large degree of disagreement on six issues, namely the "green" effect of nuclear energy, the economical aspects of nuclear energy, the safety of nuclear power plants, the management of radioactive waste, the supply of uranium and the public perception of nuclear energy.

1. Environmental Impact of Nuclear Energy

The first source of debate concerns the environmental impact of the use of nuclear energy. Nuclear industry refers to the proven fact that nuclear power plants are less polluting than conventional coal plants and thus nuclear energy is one of the best ways to reduce carbon dioxide emissions. It is estimated that if all currently operating nuclear power plants in Europe were replaced by a representative mix of the other base-load sources of electricity (i.e. mainly coal and gas-fired plants) then roughly an additional 700 million tonnes of CO_2 would be emitted each year - equivalent to that produced by all private cars in Europe.[4] As such, nuclear energy is said to contribute to the fight against global warming.

On the other hand, anti-nuclear opposition questions the positive environmental effects of nuclear power plants pointing to the fact

---

[4] EC, DG Research & Innovation "*Fission at glance*", available from
http://ec.europa.eu/research/energy/euratom/fission/at-a-glance/index_en.htm

that the activities supporting nuclear energy generation cause considerable CO_2 pollution - for example transport, mining, etc.

2. Economics of Nuclear Energy

The second point of discussion relates to the economics of nuclear power generation. Over the last years, the lower operational costs and increased capacity utilisation of nuclear power plants have improved the competitiveness of nuclear energy. As a result, the nuclear electricity is currently one of the cheapest forms of electricity on some markets. A report by the OECD Nuclear Energy Agency and International Energy Agency indicates that the cost of generating nuclear energy, at a 5% discount rate, lies between 29 and 82 USD/MWh whilst generating electricity from coal-fired and gas-fired power plants costs between 54 and 120 USD/MWh and between 67 and 105 USD/MWh respectively.[5] It is also indicated that at a 5% discount rate, the average generation costs for onshore and offshore wind power plants vary between 75 USD/MWh and 175 USD/MWh, whereas the cost of generating solar energy can go up to 215 USD/MWh. Furthermore, the International Energy Agency confirms that "shifting away from nuclear power can have significant implications for a country's spending on imports of fossil fuels and for electricity prices".[6]

---

[5] OECD Nuclear Energy Agency and International Energy Agency *"Projected costs of Generating Electricity"* (2010), pp. 23-24, available from *http://www.iea.org/textbase/nppdf/free/2010/projected_costs.pdf*
[6] International Energy Agency *"World Energy Outlook 2012"*, published in November 2012, p. 6.

However, it has been argued that the economics of nuclear energy may not be all that optimistic, because in deregulated markets nuclear power is not fully cost competitive with coal and natural gas.[7] Capital costs of building a nuclear plant are two to three times higher compared to traditional coal plants, which also take less time to construct. Additionally, the costs of building a new nuclear plant - fuel costs, raw materials, interest rates - are continuously rising and there is also a lack of skilled staff. Therefore, it can be claimed that the nuclear industry survives thanks to subsidies. Furthermore, the association between nuclear power plants and politics, as well as in many cases the blurred legal framework, make nuclear installations to be considered as highly uncertain investments. According to the International Energy Agency, nuclear energy will only be cost-effective "if the governments of countries where nuclear power is accepted play a stronger role in facilitating private investments, especially in liberalised markets".[8]

3. Safety of Nuclear Energy

Safety of nuclear power plants is one of the fundamental problems of nuclear energy. As it has been recently seen in Fukushima, a meltdown of a nuclear reactor can have tremendous consequences. Such a nuclear accident bears the risk of causing many victims, not only immediately after the accident and in the surroundings of the reactor but also many

---

[7] See Massachusetts Institute of Technology "Update of the MIT Future of Nuclear Energy - an Interdisciplinary MIT Study" (2009), available from http://web.mit.edu/nuclearpower/pdf/nuclearpower-update2009.pdf
[8] Ross McCracken "Nuclear Growth Faces Supply-side Constraints" (2006), Energy Economist, Issue 297, p. 6.

years later and relatively far away from the place of accident. It would also have disastrous consequences for the environment. It is worth mentioning that up until Fukushima nuclear meltdown, nuclear supporters emphasised that only two major accidents had taken place - at Three Mile island in 1979 and in Chernobyl in 1986, largely due to low safety standards and since then nuclear power plants have been much better protected. However, as it has been seen, accidents can be never excluded, particularly not as a consequence of *force majeure* circumstances, and the risk of potential terrorist attacks must be taken into consideration. Furthermore, there has been a number of recent, small-scaled accidents in Sweden, where one reactor's back-up system failed, and in Spain, where regulators imposed a fine of EUR 1.6 million to a plant due to poor maintenance.[9]

4. Management of Radioactive Waste

The fourth point of controversy relates to the management of radioactive waste produced during the process of nuclear energy generation. The most updated classification of radioactive waste was set out in the IAEA Safety Guide issued in 2009.[10] However, in its most recent Situation Report on Radioactive Waste issued in 2011,[11] the Commission did not take into account the IAEA

---

[9] *"Reacting Badly to Summer heat - Heavy Weather for Europe's Nuclear plants"* (2006), The Economist, 10 August 2006, available from *http://www.economist.com/node/7281129*
[10] International Atomic Energy Agency *"Classification of Radioactive Waste"*, General Safety Guide, Vienna (2009), available from *http://www-pub.iaea.org/MTCD/publications/PDF/Pub1419_web.pdf*
[11] EC *"Seventh Situation Report on Radioactive Waste and Spent Fuel Management in the European Union"* SEC (2011) 1007, 22 August 2011, available from *http://ec.europa.eu/energy/nuclear/waste_management/doc/seventh_situation_report_corr_version_without_cover_page.pdf*

scheme for classification of radioactive waste since the reference date for the inventories was 2007.

The first two categories established by the IAEA are Exempt Waste (EW) and Very Short Lived Waste (VSLW). EW is waste with such a low radioactivity content that it does not require controlling by regulatory authorities. Once the material is cleared by the national regulatory authority it is no longer considered as radioactive waste. VSLW is waste that can be stored for a limited period of up to a few years to allow its radioactivity content to reduce by radioactive decay. It can subsequently be cleared from regulatory control according to arrangements approved by domestic regulatory authorities for disposal as ordinary waste, for use or for controlled discharge. This class includes waste containing radionuclides with very short half-lives often used for research and medical purposes. Those two categories have not been reported on by the Commission.

The third category set out by the IAEA - Very Low Level Waste (VLLW) – usually has higher radioactivity content than EW but may, nonetheless, not need a high level of containment and isolation. It is suitable for disposal in near-surface landfill type facilities with limited regulatory control. Typical waste in this class includes soil and rubble with low levels of radioactivity which originate from sites formerly contaminated by radioactivity. It may also contain small amounts of longer-lived radionuclides. This waste category does not necessarily exist in all Member States. The reasons for this are that it may not be cost-effective to demonstrate compliance with clearance levels or there may be issues of public concern regarding the release of such materials. The annual generation of VLLW in the EU amounts to 30 700 m³.[12]

The fourth category, Low Level Waste (LLW), has high radioactivity content but contains limited amounts of long-lived radionuclides with half-lives of less than 30 years and for which there is negligible heat generation as a result of radioactive decay. It requires robust isolation and containment for periods of up to few hundred years and is suitable for disposal in engineered or near-surface repositories. It covers a very broad range of waste and may include short-lived radionuclides at higher levels of activity concentration, and also long-lived radionuclides, but only at relatively low levels of activity concentration. The Commission categorised this waste as Low and Intermediate Level Waste – Short-Lived (LILW-SL), 40 900 m³ of which is produced every year in the EU.[13]

The fifth category, Intermediate Level Waste (ILW), requires a greater degree of containment and isolation than that provided by near surface disposal due to its radioactivity content, particularly of long-lived radionuclides. ILW also produces negligible thermal power but has a concentration of long half-life radionuclides above the limit for classification as LLW. Therefore, ILW requires disposal at greater depths, of the order of tens of metres to a few hundred metres. In the EU, there is currently no such disposal facility in operation. The Commission categorised

---

[12] *Ibid.*, p 8.
[13] *Ibid.*

the waste in this class as Low and Intermediate Level Waste – Long-Lived (LILW-LL), 38 900 m^3 of which is generated annually.[14]

The sixth category set out by both the IAEA and the Commission is High Level Waste (HLW). This is waste with levels of activity concentration high enough to generate significant quantities of heat by the radioactive decay process or waste with large amounts of long-lived radionuclides. HLW is produced by nuclear reactors and contains fission products and transuranic elements generated in the reactor core. Disposal in deep, stable geological formations usually several hundred metres or more below the surface is the generally recognised option for its disposal. HLW accounts for over 95 percent of the total radioactivity produced in the process of nuclear electricity generation. In the EU, 190 m^3 is generated per year, all of which requires long-term storage.[15] However, no deep underground disposal facility in operation exists in the EU yet.

Considering the above, it can be seen that about 110 070 m^3 of radioactive waste is produced every year in the EU. Furthermore, the total quantity of waste that has been disposed of by the end of 2007 amounts to 2 149 200 m^3.[16] Since there is still no disposal facility in operation available for the last three and most hazardous categories of radioactive waste in the EU, these types of waste remain currently stored in temporary surface and near-surface storage facilities in the Member States with active or past nuclear power programmes. It is estimated that the quantities of

---

[14] *Ibid.*
[15] *Ibid.*, p 9.
[16] *Ibid.*, p 6.

radioactive waste in storage at the end of 2007 amount to 221 500 m^3 (LLW), 287 000 m^3 (ILW) and 4 100 m^3 (HLW).[17]

The geological disposal requires the radioactive waste to be stored by isolation at several hundred of metres depth in stable rock environment and so far, this process has not been put into practice - its financing still remains uncertain and many environmentalists strongly reject it. In addition, most Member States have adopted low-level, short-lived waste policies. However, nowadays, there seems to be movement towards a consensus about the benefits of geological disposal. In November 2009, a Technology Platform for Implementing Geological Disposal (IGD-TP) of nuclear waste was launched with the support of the Commission[18] and since then, radioactive waste management organisations in Sweden, Finland and France, together with the German Federal Ministry of Economics and Technology, have piloted the setting up of this Technological Platform. The founding members are waste management organisations in Belgium (ONDRAF/NIRAS), Finland (Posiva), France (Andra), Spain (ENRESA), Sweden (SKB), Switzerland (Nagra) and UK (NDA), and the German Federal Ministry of Economics and Technology (BMWi). The IGD-TP lays down the technical steps needed within the next 10-15 years to implement geological disposal of nuclear waste in those Member States with the most advanced national programme. These will be the world's first geological repositories for high-level and long-lived

[17] Ibid., p 12.
[18] EC, DG Research & Innovation "Technology Platform for Implementing Geological Disposal launched", Press Release, 12 November 2009, available from http://ec.europa.eu/research/index.cfm?pg=newsalert&lg=en&year=2009&na=na-121109-2

nuclear waste. Progress has been made in Finland, Sweden and France where sites have been selected accompanied by plans to commission those geological repositories at latest by 2025.[19]

5. Supply of Uranium

Uranium - the basic fuel for nuclear plants is not widely found in Europe; hence the EU depends on its importation from third countries such as USA, Canada, Australia, Russia, Kazakhstan, Niger, South Africa and Namibia. In 2011, natural uranium supplies to the EU continued to come from diversified sources, Russia, Canada and Kazakhstan being top three countries of origin and providing 59 % of the natural uranium delivered to the EU.[20] Taking into consideration that those counties are reliable partners of the EU and the fact that there is no single country dominating the market, it can be concluded that the EU's uranium supply is relatively guaranteed.

On the other hand, concerns have been raised about the availability of uranium ore in long term. Current uranium supply is sufficient to meet the demand in Europe in short and medium terms, but there is no certain prediction how long the uranium ore reserves will last. This uncertainty may negatively affect the viability of nuclear energy.

---

[19] See Implementing Geological Disposal of Radioactive Waste Technology Platform *"Deployment Plan 2011–2016"* (2012), available from *http://www.igdtp.eu/Documents/EU-rapport%20deployment%20plan%20webb.pdf*
[20] Euratom Supply Agency *"Annual Report"* (2012), pp. 24-25, available from *http://ec.europa.eu/euratom/ar/last.pdf*

6. Public Opinion

Public perception of nuclear energy is the final main element of the nuclear debate. Since the accident in Chernobyl in 1986, public opinion has been very suspicious of nuclear power and the recent nuclear meltdown in Fukushima has broadened the opposition against the use of nuclear energy. A Eurobarometer survey, concluded in 2010, illustrates that the majority of EU citizens oppose nuclear power, even though the European public opinion accepts the value of nuclear energy, primarily as an instrument of decreasing energy dependence.[21] 17% favoured an increase in the level of use of nuclear energy whilst 39% of the respondents stated that the current level should be maintained. In addition, 34% of Europeans claimed that the use of nuclear energy should be reduced.

It can be also noted that public acceptance of nuclear energy varies from one Member State to another. The highest proportions of EU citizens who say that the share of nuclear energy should be increased are found in Poland (30%) and Estonia (29%), while large numbers of respondents who would like to maintain the proportion of nuclear energy at the current level are found in Finland (51%), Belgium (51%), Slovenia (51%) and France (45%). 66% of Hungarians, 65% of Greeks and 52% of Germans claimed that the share of nuclear energy should be reduced. The Eurobarometer survey also showed that

---

[21] See *"Europeans and Nuclear Safety"* (2010), Special Eurobarometer 324 / Wave 72.2 – TNS Opinion & Social, available from *http://ec.europa.eu/energy/nuclear/safety/doc/2010_eurobarometer_safety.pdf*

74% of the EU citizens feel that they have not been well informed on the issues of nuclear safety.

III. Current Status of Nuclear Energy in the EU

1. Nuclear Energy in the EU as a Whole

Figure 1: *Share of primary energy sources in the EU - 27 (2011)*
Share of primary energy sources in the EU - 27 (2011)
(Source: Eurostat - April 2012)

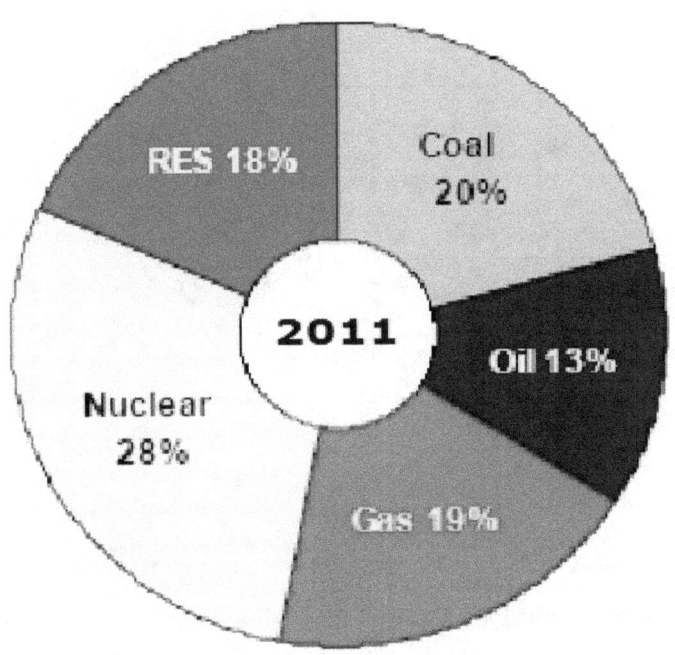

The use of nuclear energy in the EU as a primary energy source has been growing steadily over the years to reach a share of 28% in the total energy consumption for the year 2011.

Figure 2: *Share of electricity generation in the EU - 27 (2011)*
Share of electricity generation in the EU - 27 (2011)
(Source: Eurostat - April 2012)

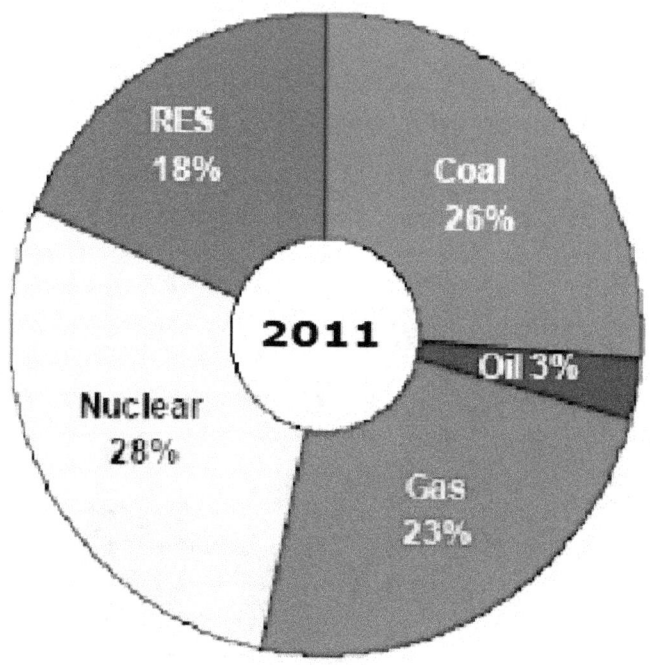

The share of electricity generated by nuclear power in the EU is 28% whilst coal is being responsible for 26%, gas for 23% and oil for 3%. The share of electricity generated by renewable energy sources amount to 18%.

2. Nuclear Energy in the Member States

Presently, fourteen Members States operate nuclear power plants: Belgium, Bulgaria, Czech Republic, Finland, France, Germany, Hungary, the Netherlands, Romania, Slovenia, Slovakia, Spain, Sweden and the United Kingdom. Among these "nuclear" Member States, the importance of nuclear energy in the national energy mix varies widely. In France (77.7%), Slovakia (55.2%) and Belgium (51.5%), the share of nuclear energy is highest. France (58) also has the largest number of nuclear reactors in its territory, followed by the United Kingdom (16) and Sweden (10).

Table 1: The number of existing, under construction and planned nuclear reactors and the share of electricity generated by nuclear power (Sources: Word Nuclear Association, December 2012; OECD Nuclear Energy Data, published in October 2012)

Member State	Number of operational nuclear power reactors	Planned /proposed nuclear power reactors	Share of electricity generated by nuclear power
Belgium	7	-	51.5%
Bulgaria	2	1	35%
Czech Republic	6	2	32%
Finland	4 + 1 under construction	2	31.6%
France	58 + 1 under construction	1	77.7%
Germany	9	-	17.5%
Hungary	4	2	43.2%
Lithuania Latvia Estonia	-	2 (joint ownership)	-
Netherlands	1	2	3.6%
Poland	-	5	-
Romania	2	2	10%
Slovakia	4 + 2 under construction	-	55.2%
Slovenia Croatia	1 (joint ownership)	1 (fully owned by Slovenia)	38.5% 15%
Spain	8	-	19.5%
Sweden	10	-	39.6%
United Kingdom	16	12	19 %
Total EU – 28 (including Croatia)	132 + 4 under construction	32	28.3 %

Table 2: Position towards the use of nuclear energy by the "nuclear" Members States
(Sources: World Nuclear Association, December 2012; OECD Nuclear Energy Data, published in October 2012)

Member State	Position towards the use of nuclear energy
Belgium	Construction of new nuclear plants prohibited and phase-out policy decided in 2003 by the Belgian Senate. 2 reactors will be shut down in 2015 and 1 by 2025 whereas the closure period for the rest 4 reactors has been extended beyond 2025.
Bulgaria	4 reactors have been closed in the context of accession negotiations. Construction of a new nuclear plant (2 reactors) in Belene was planned, but subsequently cancelled and instead, a third 1000 MWe unit will be added to the present plant in Kozloduy.
Czech Republic	Government's commitment to the future of nuclear energy is strong. 2 new nuclear reactors are planned to be built.
Finland	Government committed to nuclear power - a fifth reactor is now under construction and 2 more are planned.
France	Strong commitment to nuclear energy - the country has been very active in developing nuclear technology. Reactors and fuel products and services are a major export. France is building its first Generation III reactor and is planning a second one.
Germany	A coalition government formed after the 1998 federal elections had the phasing out of nuclear energy as a feature of its policy. With a new government in 2009, the phase-out was cancelled, but then reintroduced in 2011, with 8 reactors shut down immediately. Public opinion in Germany remains ambivalent and at present does not support building new nuclear plants.
Hungary	The Hungarian Parliament has expressed overwhelming support for building 2 new nuclear power reactors.
Lithuania Latvia Estonia	Lithuania closed its last nuclear reactor, which had been generating 70% of its electricity, at the end of 2009. A new nuclear plant (2 units) is planned to be built together with other Baltic states. In October 2011, the government formally notified the European Commission. Initially Poland also participated in the project, but withdrew in December 2011.
Netherlands	A previous decision to phase out nuclear power has been reversed. Public and political support is increasing for expanding nuclear energy. 2 new units have been proposed.

Poland	Poland's Energy Policy until 2030, developed by the Polish Ministry of Economy in 2009, sets out measures aimed at creating a legal framework and organisational structure for the development of a nuclear programme. The government issued a statement on its plans to build a power plant (1 unit) entering in operation in 2022 and second one (4 units) in 2030. In 2010, the best sites for nuclear power plants were chosen.
Romania	Romanian government's support for nuclear energy is strong. Plans are well advanced for completing 2 more units, but finance is lacking.
Slovakia	Government's commitment to the future of nuclear energy is strong. Slovakia has 4 nuclear reactors generating half of its electricity and 2 more under construction.
Slovenia Croatia	Slovenia has shared a nuclear power reactor in Krsko with Croatia since 1981. It is owned and operated by GEN Energija - a joint Slovene-Croat company. A further Krsko unit is under consideration and it would be fully owned by Slovenia.
Spain	Moratorium and phase-out policy since 1984. Government's commitment to the future of nuclear energy has remained uncertain, but has firmed up as the cost of subsidising renewables becomes unaffordable.
Sweden	Referendum in 1980 against nuclear power. Phasing-out programmes delayed several time. In June 2010, the Parliament approved the government's decision to abolish the act banning construction of new nuclear reactors, as well as a survey showed overall 72% public support for the government's decision to allow building of new reactors. However, any new units, if required, will be built after 2025.
United Kingdom	The government assumes there will be a requirement of 60 GWe of new generating capacity by 2025, of which 35 GWe is to come from renewables whilst the expectation is for "a significant proportion" of the remaining 25 GWe to come from nuclear, although the government has not set a fixed target for nuclear capacity. Since the government reversed its unfavourable policy towards nuclear in 2006, 12 new nuclear reactors have been proposed and planned.

The Member States of the EU are much divided over the use of nuclear energy. Sixteen countries from the table above continue or have the intention to develop nuclear energy programmes whereas only three "nuclear" Member States – Belgium, Germany and Spain - have adopted a phasing-out policy.

On the other hand, the remaining nine "non-nuclear" Member States – Austria, Cyprus, Denmark, Greece, Ireland, Italy, Luxembourg, Malta and Portugal – oppose and have no plans to build any nuclear energy reactors (*Table 3*). However, it is worth pointing out that Denmark, Italy and Greece import electricity generated by nuclear power.

Table 3: Position towards the use of nuclear energy by the "non-nuclear" Members States
(Sources: World Nuclear Association, December 2012; OECD Nuclear Energy Data, published in October 2012)

Member State	Position towards the use of nuclear energy
Austria	Nuclear power has been banned in Austria since late 1978. In 1999, this ban became part of constitutional legislation (Federal Constitutional Act "Atomfreies Österreich", Federal Law Gazette 149/1999). The Austrian position regarding nuclear power has been underlined by the Fukushima accident. The government continue to pursue an active policy in this regard.
Cyprus	Cyprus does not use and does not plan to introduce nuclear power in its energy mix in the foreseeable future.
Denmark	Denmark was once at the forefront of nuclear research and had planned on building nuclear power plants. However, in 1985, the Danish parliament passed a resolution that nuclear power plants would not be built in the country and there is currently no move to reverse this situation. About ten percent of domestic consumption is from nuclear power, imported from Sweden and Germany.

Greece	Although Greece has established a national Atomic Energy Commission a decision has been made not to implement nuclear power program to generate electricity. The country believes that due to its small size and frequent earthquakes in the region, nuclear power would not provide many benefits. Greece did receive electricity produced by nuclear power from Bulgaria in the past. However, with the shutdown of 2 Bulgarian reactors in 2006, these imports are almost non-existent.
Ireland	In 1968, a nuclear power plant (4 reactors) was proposed to be built during the 1970s, but the plan was dropped in 1981 after strong opposition from environmentalist groups. In April 2006, a government-commissioned report by Forfás pointed to the need for Ireland to reconsider nuclear power in order "to secure its long-run energy security". In 2007, Ireland's Electricity Supply Board made it known that it would consider a joint venture with a major EU energy company to build nuclear capacity. However, following the 2011 Fukushima nuclear disaster, Ireland has become strongly anti-nuclear.
Italy	Italy has had four operating nuclear power reactors but shut the last two down in 1990 following the Chernobyl accident. In 2008, government's policy towards nuclear changed and a substantial new nuclear build program was planned. However, in a June 2011 referendum the 2009 legislation setting up arrangements to generate 25% of the country's electricity from nuclear power by 2030 was rejected. Some 10% of its electricity is now from nuclear power – all imported.
Luxembourg	Luxembourg has had a non-nuclear policy and does not have a nuclear power programme.
Malta	Malta does not have a nuclear power programme and has no plans to develop one in the future.
Portugal	Portugal does not have a nuclear power programme and has no plans to develop one in the future.

IV. EU Nuclear Policy

1. Euratom Treaty

In 1957, the six founding Member States decided to pool their nuclear energy activities in developing what was at that time considered to be the energy source of the future by the Treaty establishing the European Atomic Energy Community, commonly referred to as the Euratom Treaty.[22] The Treaty provides the regulatory framework for the EU's nuclear activities aiming to create the necessary conditions for the establishment of nuclear industry, such as the creation of a common nuclear market and the continuous supply of nuclear materials. It also ensures the protection of workers and public via imposition of uniform health and safety standards. Furthermore, the Euratom Treaty promotes nuclear research and dissemination of information, as well as peaceful use of nuclear power. Since its adoption, the fundamental provisions of the Treaty have remained largely unchained, except for some minor institutional amendments.

It can be said that over the years the success of the Euratom Treaty has been very limited, particularly in comparison with the dynamic evolution of the other founding EU treaties. Unlike the Treaty establishing the European Coal and Steel Community (ECSC Treaty), which in 2002 automatically expired after fifty years, the Euratom treaty has no expiry date. It was argued that the difference between the two treaties can be explained though

---

[22] *Consolidated version of the Treaty establishing the European Atomic Energy Community*, Official Journal C 84 of 30 March 2010, available from *http://eur-lex.europa.eu/LexUriServ/LexUriServ.do?uri=OJ:C:2010:084:0001:0112:EN:PDF*

their diverse philosophy: the ECSC Treaty and those that followed it are market-oriented whilst the Euratom Treaty is essentially dirigiste and promotional.[23] As it was seen in the previous chapter, the Member States usually strongly disagree when it comes to nuclear energy issues – the diversity of national interests as well as the different political and economical approaches towards nuclear power have significantly increased the restrictive interpretation of the Euratom Treaty by the Member States and the EU institutions. The limited application of the Euratom Treaty has been further reinforced because it did not address certain key issues such as the operational safety of nuclear plants, the radioactive waste storage and the disposal facilities. As a result, the Member States have developed and implemented their own regulatory activities in those fields.

However, it is worth mentioning that the Euratom Treaty has achieved a solid success in relation to certain nuclear energy issues such as the introduction of uniform safety standards on radiation protection after the Chernobyl disaster and obligations for the Eastern European Member States, who joined after 2004, to either comply with certain safety standards regarding nuclear installations or to shut down their Soviet-type nuclear reactors.

1.1 Euratom Supply Agency

The Euratom Supply Agency, established by the Euratom Treaty, became operational on 1 June 1960. The Agency is located in

---

[23] Thomas F. Gusack "*A Tale of Two Treaties: An Assessment of the Euratom Treaty in Relation to the EC Treaty*" (2003), Common Market Law Review, Volume 40, pp. 117 - 141.

Luxembourg and has a legal personality and financial autonomy, but operates under the supervision of the Commission.[24] It is assisted by an Advisory Committee, which is established by the statutes of the Agency. It comprises 51 representatives proposed by Member States and appointed by the Council of the EU from amongst producers, users and experts (government or private sector).

In general, the Agency ensures the regular and equitable supply of nuclear fuels for EU users. The Euratom Treaty authorises the Supply Agency to acquire ores, source material and special fissile material produced in the EU and gives it an exclusive right to conclude contracts for the supply of such materials from inside or outside of the EU. Given that in most supplier countries public authorities are involved in the contractual activities of nuclear fuel supply companies, the Agency acts as a kind of counterweight to public authority involvement in the supplier countries, in order to avoid undue constraints with regard to the use or further circulation being imposed. It also provides expertise, information and advice on the nuclear market and monitors trends of the market in nuclear materials and services which could affect the security of supply.

The Court of Justice of the EU had an opportunity to review the exclusive rights of the Supply Agency by stating "where decisions concerning economic and commercial policy and nuclear policy

---

[24] Council Decision 2008/114/EC, Euratom of 12 February 2008 establishing Statutes for the Euratom Supply Agency, Official Journal L 41 of 15 February 2008.

are concerned, the Agency has a broad discretion when exercising its powers"; however   the Court acknowledged its power to "identifying any manifestly wrong assessment or misuse of power" by the Agency.[25]

It has been stated that the Euratom supply system, which was designed to be a monopolistic system, has been implemented in a simplified fashion, without abandoning any of its objectives or main tools.[26] Therefore, it was possible to deal with new market difficulties in a flexible way, without undue rigidity. Furthermore, with the accession of new Member States to the EU, the generous transitional regime of the system has permitted the continuation of the existing supply arrangements and thus has avoided major disruptions of the traditional supply patterns.

1.2 Euratom Loan Facility (Euratom Lending Instrument)

Next aspect of the EU's nuclear policy concerns the Euratom Loan Facility, also known as the Euratom Lending Instrument. In 1977, the Council of the EU empowered the Commission to provide long-term financing (in the form of loans) to "projects relating to the industrial production of electricity in nuclear power stations and industrial fuel cycle installations" in the EU Member States.[27]

---

[25] Court of First Instance Judgement of 15 October 1995, cases T-458/93 and T-523/93, *ENU v. Commission,*
ECR 1995, p. II 2459, point 67; appeal against this judgement was rejected by the Court of Justice in its
Judgement of 11 March 1997, case C-337/95P, *ENU v. Commission*, ECR 1997, p. I 1329.
[26] See André Bouquet "*How Current are Euratom Provisions on Nuclear Supply and Ownership in View of the European Union's Enlargement?*" (2001), Nuclear Law Bulletin No. 68, pp 7-38.
[27] Council Decision 77/270/Euratom of 29 March 1977, Official Journa L 88, 6 April 1977, p. 9.

The Loan Facility was established in a context of rising oil prices and amid growing concerns about Europe's excessive dependence on energy imports. During the period from 1977 to 1987, the Euratom Loan Facility co-financed the construction of nine nuclear power plants, a uranium enrichment plant and a uranium reprocessing facility in five Member States (Belgium, France, Germany, Italy and the United Kingdom).[28] The total loan amount of EUR 2 876 million has been fully repaid by the borrowers. No Euratom loans have been granted for investment projects in the Member States since February 1987.

Following the Chernobyl reactor accident in 1986, the scope of the Euratom Lending Instrument was extended in 1994 to cover the financing of projects designed "to improve the safety and efficiency of nuclear facilities" in certain third countries of the Central and Eastern Europe Community and of the Commonwealth of Independent States.[29] Since 1994 the Commission has granted three Euratom loans: EUR 223.5 million for the safety upgrade of Kozloduy 5 and 6 (Bulgaria) in April 2000, EUR 212.5 million for the completion to an adequate safety level of unit 2 at Cernavoda (Romania) in March 2004 and USD 83 million for the safety upgrade of Khmelnitsky 2 and Rovno 4 (Ukraine) in July 2004.[30]

---

[28] EC, DG Economic and financial Affairs "*Ex-Post Evaluation of the Euratom Loan Facility*" 3 June 2011, p. iv, available from http://ec.europa.eu/economy_finance/evaluation/pdf/report_evaluation_loan_facility_en.pdf
[29] Council decision 94/179/Euratom of 21 March 1994 amending Decision 77/270/Euratom, to authorise the Commission to contract Euratom borrowings in order to contribute to the financing required for improving the degree of efficiency and safety of nuclear power stations in certain non-member countries, OJ L84, 29 March 1994, p. 41.
[30] EC, DG Economic and financial Affairs "*Ex-Post Evaluation of the Euratom Loan Facility*" 3 June 2011, p. Iv.

Currently, Russia, Armenia and Ukraine are the only third countries which are eligible for Euratom loans. The financial support is limited to 20 per cent of the total project cost for the Member States and 50 per cent of the cost of "safety and efficiency" measures for third countries. Euratom loans are "off-budget" operations which the Commission finances "back to back" by borrowing from the financial markets. The Facility is subject to a cumulative ceiling of EUR 4 billion as the current amount available for new loans within this ceiling is EUR 626 million. Since its inception, the Euratom Lending Instrument has provided long term loans for the amount of EUR 3.4 billion to nuclear projects in the EU and its neighbouring countries.[31]

Over the years, the Euratom Loan Facility has been criticised due to a number of problems. It was argued that the European Investment Bank, which assesses the economics of the projects did not lend its own resources for nuclear power plants or lend in the Commonwealth of Independent States region at all, and thus had obtained little experience in assessing nuclear projects or in that region in general.[32] In addition, neither the Member States nor the Parliament have been involved in the individual project assessment decisions since they were not presented in the Cabinet of the Commissioners - the body responsible for approving the loan decisions. Finally, the opponents of nuclear energy also express strong criticism of the Lending Instrument because it, according to them, unfairly favours nuclear power at

---

[31] *Ibid*.
[32] Antony Froggatt *"The Extension of the Euratom Loan Ceiling: An Opportunity for Euratom Reform"* September 2002, p. 2, available from *http://www.eu-energy.com/pdfs/extensioneuratomloanceiling.pdf*

the expense of other technologies which do not have their own loan facilities.

Nowadays, the Commission recommends various measures in order to ensure the efficient continuity of the Euratom Loan Facility and its ability to address clearly identified financing gaps.[33] There is no need for the Facility to support investment in front-end fuel cycle facilities anymore; it should direct the Euratom Loans available to the safety upgrades and improvements within the EU. Accordingly, the legal framework should be amended in order to reflect the distinct intervention logics for investment in new builds (including demonstrator reactors) and safety upgrades/improvements.[34] Financing of large scale research and development infrastructures (such as commercial scale demonstration reactors) should be also considered in the absence of any corresponding EU financing instrument. Furthermore, a new lending limit amounting to EUR 10 billion is proposed in order for the anticipated financing needs of the nuclear sector to be met. Lastly, the visibility and transparency of the Euratom Loan Facility should be improved through systematic dissemination of information regarding the Facility as the information package should reflect the needs of the different stakeholder groups (EU citizens, industry players and policy makers).

---

[33] EC, DG Economic and financial Affairs "*Ex-Post Evaluation of the Euratom Loan Facility*" 3 June 2011, p. 92, available from http://ec.europa.eu/economy_finance/evaluation/pdf/report_evaluation_loan_facility_en.pdf
[34] *Ibid.*, It is recommended that those two purposes should be adopted by two separate Council Decisions.

1.3 Nuclear Illustrative Programmes under Euratom (PINCs)

In accordance with Article 40 of the Euratom Treaty, the Commission has regularly published Nuclear Illustrative Programmes, also known as PINCs.[35] PINCs aim to provide information on nuclear energy in the EU, the objectives adopted by the Member States for nuclear power production and the investment required for their attainment. The first three PINCs were published in 1966, 1972 and 1984 and focused on production targets. The drafting of the fourth illustrative program was accompanied with many complications as Members States had developed contradictory views on nuclear energy in the wake of the Chernobyl accident. This divergence was clearly addressed in the 1995 Commission's White Paper on Energy Policy: "a number of Member States depend to a large extent on nuclear energy, whilst others prefer to pursue a non-nuclear energy policy, and a third group have decided to reduce dependency on nuclear-based sources of energy or to terminate the existing nuclear-plants altogether".[36] When the fourth PINC was finally adopted in 1997, it confirmed that nuclear power is a highly controversial issue in the EU with many different views being expressed in a context of varying energy structures and approaches to nuclear energy.[37]

---

[35] PINC stands for "*Programme Indicatif Nucleaire pour la Communaute*".

[36] EC "*White Paper: An Energy Policy for the European Union*" COM(95) 682, 13 December 1995, pp. 84-85, available from *http://europa.eu/documentation/official-docs/white-papers/pdf/energy_white_paper_com_95_682.pdf*

[37] See "*Communication from the Commission on the Nuclear Industries in the European Union. An illustrative Programme According to Article 40 on the Euratom Treaty*", 25 September 1997, COM (97) 401, available from *http://aei.pitt.edu/6258/1/6258.pdf*

In 2007, the Commission presented the fifth and latest PINC.[38] It underlined the significant contribution of nuclear energy in the EU's energy mix, its importance as a carbon dioxide free energy source, as well as its crucial role to the main priorities identified by the Commission[39] towards competitive, sustainable and secure energy. The Commission also laid down five conditions for the acceptance of nuclear energy, namely a favourable public opinion, nuclear safety, a solution for the disposal of radioactive waste, decommissioning and radiological protection.

1.4 Framework Programmes (FPs)

As it was mentioned above, the promotion of nuclear research was one of the objectives of the Euratom Treaty. Before 1984, the EU's research and development (R&D) activities, including nuclear research, were carried out using a case-by-case approach. Since then these R&D activities have been integrated into comprehensive and multi-annual schemes known as Framework Programmes (FP). The first Framework Programme (FP1 - with a budget of EUR 3.75 billion) covered the period 1984-87, the second (FP2 - EUR 5.396 billion) the period 1987-91, the third (FP3 - EUR 6.6 billion) the period 1991-94, the fourth (FP4 - EUR 13.215 billion) the period 1994-98, the fifth (FP5 - EUR 14.96 billion) the period 1998-2002 and the sixth

---

[38] EC Communication *"Nuclear Illustrative Programme"* COM(2007) 565 final, 4 October 2007, available from *http://eur-lex.europa.eu/LexUriServ/LexUriServ.do?uri=COM:2007:0565:FIN:EN:PDF*
[39] In its Green Paper "*A European Strategy for Sustainable, Competitive and Secure Energy*" (COM 2006 105, 8 March 2006) the Commission identifies six priorities: competitiveness and the internal energy market, diversification of the internal energy mix, solidarity in the Union, sustainable development, innovation and technology, and external policies.

(FP6 - EUR 17.883 billion) the period 2002-06. The current seventh Framework Programme (FP7 - EUR 50.521 billion) covers the period 2007-13, whereas next Framework Programme will be established for the period 2014-20 under the name Horizon 2020 with an estimated budget of EUR 80 billion. Nuclear energy research has been included in successive FPs since 1984.

In the beginning, nuclear-related research was a combination of research on radioactive waste management, nuclear safety and radiation protection. However, the balance between these topics has changed over the years. Looking at the nuclear research over the FPs, it can be noted that there has been a measure of stability in areas such as safety, radiation protection and safeguards, which correspond to the tasks entrusted to the EU by the Euratom Treaty. This is particularly true for the safeguard research, where the Joint Research Centre (JRC) plays a significant role, and for the radiation protection, which provides the scientific foundation that is needed for the basic EU safety standards.

Some nuclear research activities have been increased due to the influence of changing policy needs and interests. For example, waste management has received a lot of attention and been broadened since 1994 (FP4) to include innovative topics such as partitioning and transmutations or new concepts aimed at minimising the use of the energy content of nuclear fuels.[40] On the other hand, other areas have been discontinued - this is the

---

[40] Domenico Rossetti, Bruno Schmitz, Wiktor Raldow and Michel Poireu *"European Union Energy Research"* (2007) Revue de l'Energie, No 576, March - April 2007, p. 82.

case for decommissioning research that has produced mature and well-mastered technologies and approaches; consequently, the support for dissemination of knowledge in this field has been reduced.[41]

2. EU position towards main nuclear issues

Over the years the EU has focused on a number of nuclear issues such as the safety of nuclear plants, the management of radioactive waste and the decommissioning of old nuclear facilities. It can be noted that despite the differences between the Member States, the EU's position in regard to those issues has gradually developed from a "soft" approach to legislative harmonization.

2.1 Nuclear safety policy

Safety of nuclear plants has always been a central element of the EU's nuclear policy, but because the Euratom Treaty did not explicitly address this issue, no common rules could be adopted. As a result, for several years there was no EU activity directly dealing with nuclear installation safety. However, during the 1970s, it became clear that a degree of convergence was necessary at European level to support and guide the efforts of the Member States towards harmonisation of requirements and safety criteria. Since then, a non-binding EU acquis has been developed on the basis of co-operation and voluntary harmonisation.[42] It can be noted that the acquis has been

---

[41] *Ibid.*
[42] See Non-paper (29/09/2000),

founded on fundamental common principles that form the basis of Member States' nuclear safety regulations and are recognised internationally.

The prospect of EU enlargement to the East in 1990s placed nuclear safety high on the European Agenda due to concerns that nuclear plants using older Soviet technology would become part of the Union's energy sources. The EU took series of initiatives which, to a certain extent, have achieved a level of harmonization on Union level not only in regard to the candidate-countries from Central and Eastern Europe but also to existing Members States. Accordingly, at the request made by the EU in 1993-94, Bulgaria, Lithuania and Slovakia closed eight nuclear reactors in total between 2002 and 2009.[43] Subsequently, in 1999 the Cologne European Council called upon the Commission to ensure the application of high safety nuclear standards in Central and Eastern Europe[44] and in 2001 the Laeken European Council stressed the importance of monitoring the security and safety of nuclear power plants and requested regular reports on nuclear safety from Member States.[45] Furthermore, at international level, the Euratom Community acceded to the "Convention on Nuclear Safety".[46]

---

http://ec.europa.eu/energy/nuclear/safety/doc/non_binding_acquis.pdf
[43] The EU concluded Nuclear Safety Agreements with Bulgaria and Lithuania, in which both countries agreed to close four and two of their reactors respectively (those obligations were reiterated later in Lithuania and Bulgaria's accession treaty). Slovakia adopted a resolution to close two nuclear reactors.
[44] See Presidency Conclusions, Cologne European Council (3-4 June 1999), available from
http://www.consilium.europa.eu/ueDocs/cms_Data/docs/pressdata/en/ec/57886.pdf
[45] See Presidency Conclusions, Laeken European Council (14-15 December 2001), available from
http://www.consilium.europa.eu/ueDocs/cms_Data/docs/pressdata/en/ec/68827.pdf

Following those initiatives, in its 2002 Communication "Nuclear safety in European Union" the Commission took the opportunity to re-launch the idea of harmonising nuclear safety standards in the EU.[47] However, at that time, the competence of the Commission to carry out legislative initiatives in the field of nuclear installation safety was challenged; it took a judgment of the Court of Justice of the European Union to clarify this issue.[48] The Court decided that under the Euratom Treaty the competence of national authorities responsible for nuclear safety could not preclude the Commission from legislating in this respect. Following the 2002 Communications and the Court's judgment, the Commission proposed a package (also known as the "nuclear package") of three measures on the basis of the Euratom Treaty,[49] which included a proposal for a Directive on the safety of nuclear installations.[50]

The original draft for the new Directive was presented in January 2003 and identified the basic obligations and general principles during the operating lifetime and decommissioning of nuclear plants such as common safety standards and monitoring

---

[46] EC Decision 1999/813/Euratom of 16 November 1999, Official Journal L318 (11 December 1999), p. 20.

[47] EC Communication "Nuclear Safety in European Union" COM (2002) 605 final, 6 November 2002

[48] Case C-29/99, Commission v. Council, 10 December 2002, ECR I - 11221.

[49] So-called "nuclear package" consists of three legislative proposals, namely a Directive setting out basic obligations and general principles on safety of nuclear installations during operation and decommissioning; a Directive on the management of radioactive waste; and a draft Decision authorising the Commission to negotiate an agreement between Euratom and the Russian Federation on trade in nuclear materials.

[50] Proposal for a Council Directive (EURATOM) setting out basic obligations and general principles on the safety of nuclear installations, COM (2003) 32 final, 30 January 2003, available from http://eur-lex.europa.eu/LexUriServ/LexUriServ.do?uri=COM:2003:0032:FIN:EN:PDF

methods; a requirement for all Member States to establish an independent safety authority, a system of independent verification based on cross-checking by national safety authorities; and minimum criteria with regard to the creation, management and use of decommissioning funds.

Some key amendments were introduced in 2004 and the Directive was finally adopted in 2009.[51] It applies to all nuclear installations within the EU and obliges the Member States to submit a report to the Commission every 3 years on progress made with regard to nuclear safety, as well as to submit self-assessments of their national framework every 10 years. Furthermore, the Member States should ensure that their relevant personnel have the necessary expertise and skills in nuclear safety. Information on nuclear safety regulations should be also made available to the public.

It is worth mentioning that following strong opposition from Germany, the final version of the Directive does not require the Members States any longer to provide secure ring-fenced decommissioning funds. Additionally, in response to the Member States' concerns over interference from the Commission in national legislations, a new article on subsidiary was introduced in order to guarantee that the responsibility for nuclear safety remains with the authorities of the Member States. Moreover, the very slow process towards the enactment of the Directive showed

---

[51] Council Directive 2009/71/Euratom of 25 June 2009 establishing a Community Framework for the nuclear safety of nuclear installations, Official Journal L 172/18, 2 July 2009. Up to October 2012, only Poland and Portugal still not completed the implementation of the Directive.

one more time the reluctance of many Member States to pool any national control over the opening and operation of their nuclear energy industry in the interest of a European-wide regulation.

Another aspect of the nuclear safety policy concerns the obligation under Article 41 of the Euratom Treaty for Members States to ask the Commission's view on any important new investment in the nuclear sector. More than 200 investment projects since the Treaty came into force and 19 since 1997 have been notified to the Commission. The most recent of them concern the replacement of equipment in existing installations and the construction of new reactors in Finland, France and Lithuania.[52]

Lastly, it should be noted that the Member States are individually responsible for protecting the public in the event of a nuclear emergency. However, after the Chernobyl nuclear disaster the Commission set up a 24-hour notification and exchange system (ECURIE) between the competent authorities of all Member States and Switzerland.[53]

2.2 Radioactive waste policy

Radioactive waste management has been subject to certain control by the Commission since the conclusion of the Euratom

---

[52] EC Communication *"Nuclear Illustrative Programme"* COM(2007) 565 final, 4 October 2007, pp. 6-7, available from *http://eur-lex.europa.eu/LexUriServ/LexUriServ.do?uri=COM:2007:0565:FIN:EN:PDF*
[53] Council Decision of 14 December 1987 on Community arrangements for the early exchange of information in the event of a radiological emergency, Official Journal L 371, 30 December 1987, pp. 0076 - 0078. ECURIE stands for European Community Urgent Radiological Information Exchange.

Treaty. Article 37 of the Treaty obliges the Member States to provide the Commission with information in regard to any plans for disposal of radioactive waste in order for the Commission to assess the health and environmental impact of such plans on other Member States.

In 1980, the Council adopted a Community plan for action in the field of radioactive waste for the period from 1980 to 1992[54], which was renewed once until the end of 1999.[55] The plan focused on the management and storage of high activity and/or long-life waste and encouraged harmonisation and co-operation among the Member States. The Commission has also published a series of Situational Reports on waste management in the EU aiming to present the status and trends of waste management. In the seventh and most recent report, published in 2007[56], and similarly to the fifth PINC mentioned above, it was noted that the deep disposal in a stable rock formation is the preferred option by nuclear operators, whereas others prefer near-surface storage in order to make surveillance and potential recovery easier in the future if required. The Commission also pointed out that some of the main factors affecting the progress in finding solutions are socio-political rather than technical. As such, the disposal of radioactive waste should be subject to serious assessment of its

[54] Council Resolution of 10 February 1980 on the implementation of a Community Plan of action in the field of radioactive waste, Official Journal C 051, 29 February 1980.

[55] Council Resolution of 15 June 1992 on the renewal of a Community Plan of action in the field of radioactive waste, Official Journal C 158, 25 June 1992.

[56] EC Seventh Situational Report "*Radioactive waste and spent fuel management in the European Union*" Brussels, 22 August 2011 SEC(2011) 1007 final, available from
http://ec.europa.eu/energy/nuclear/waste_management/doc/seventh_situation_r eport_corr_version_without_cover_page.pdf

impact on human health and environment - a concern which was raised and strongly defended during the discussion of the proposal for a Directive on radioactive waste.

Another part of the "nuclear package", a proposal for Directive on the management of radioactive waste[57], was presented in January 2003. The proposal included requirements for safe management of spent nuclear fuel and radioactive waste including a clear preference for geological storage of waste; an obligation for all Member States to adopt national programmes for the management of radioactive waste, in accordance with a strict timetable; and provisions for more funding and cooperation between the Member States in the field of research on waste management. During the long process towards the adoption of the Directive some of the elements were changed. For instance, the absolute priority of geological disposal was removed; hence the Member States are not obliged anymore to give priority to this solution. In addition, the firm timetable for national programmes was abandoned; however the Member States are required to draft long-term national management programmes for radioactive waste and notify them to the Commission by 2015 at the latest.

The Directive was adopted in 2011[58] and applies to spent fuel management resulting from civilian activities and to radioactive

---

[57] Proposal for a Council Directive (EURATOM) on the management of spent nuclear fuel and radioactive waste, COM (2003) 32 final, 30 January 2003, available from *http://eur-lex.europa.eu/LexUriServ/LexUriServ.do?uri=COM:2003:0032:FIN:EN:PDF*

[58] Council Directive 2011/70/Euratom of 19 July 2011 establishing a Community framework for the responsible and safe management of spent fuel and radioactive waste, Official Journal L 199, 02 August 2011, pp. 48 - 56.

waste management from generation up to disposal originating from civilian activities. The Member States are responsible for the management of spent fuel and radioactive waste and, in the case of shipment of the latter to a third country, the responsibility continues to lie with the State of origin. Similarly to the Directive on safety of nuclear installations, there are requirements for information transparency and for the establishment of an independent regulatory authority that has the legal powers and financial resources necessary to carry out control, monitoring, licensing and enforcement actions in the field of spent fuel and radioactive waste management.

A number of other measures have been taken at European level, such as the creation of a Union-wide system of supervision and control of international shipments of radioactive waste.[59] Furthermore, on the basis of Article 30 of the Euratom Treaty, basic standards to protect the health of general public and workers against the dangers of ionising radiation have been adopted. First basic standards Directives were adopted in 1959[60] and subsequently have been revised on a regular basis. The most recent revision of the basic safety standards was adopted in May 1996[61], whilst the most recent proposal by the Commission was submitted in May 2012.[62]

---

[59] Council Regulation (Euratom) No 1493/93 of 8 June 1993 on shipments of radioactive substances between Member States, Official Journal L 148 , 19 June 1993, pp. 1 - 7; Council Directive 2006/117/Euratom of 20 November 2006 on the supervision and control of shipments of radioactive waste and spent fuel, Official Journal L 337, 05 December 2006, pp. 21 - 32.

[60] Directives of 2 February 1959 laying down the basic standards for the protection of the health of workers and the general public against the dangers arising from ionizing radiation, OJ No 11, 20 February 1959, pp. 211-259.

[61] Council Directive 96/29/Euratom of 13 May 1996 laying down basic safety standards for the protection of the health of workers and the general public against the dangers arising from ionizing radiation, Official Journal L 159 , 29

In an international context, the Euratom Community acceded to the "Joint Convention on the Safety of Spent Fuel Management and on the Safety Radioactive Waste Management".[63]

2.3 Decommissioning policy

Nuclear decommissioning is the final phase in the economic lifecycle of a nuclear power plant, in which it is permanently taken out of service. Decommissioning also involves the removal of fissile material and the environmental restoration of the site. Therefore, it is a very complex and expensive undertaking for the stakeholders involved. There are three ways of decommissioning. In the Immediate Dismantling (DECON) the dismantling and decontamination activities begin within a few months or years after the closure of the nuclear power plant. In the Long Term Safe Enclosure (SAFSTOR) all decommissioning activities are postponed after the final release of regulatory control (usually for a period of 40 to 60 years). In the third option, Entombment (ENTOMB), nuclear facilities are enclosed in structurally long-lived material, such as concrete, with remaining radioactive material onsite without ever removing it totally.

Considering the age profile of the nuclear reactors in the EU, the decommissioning is already a significant issue with increasing

---

June 1996 pp. 1 - 114.
[62] EC Proposal for a Council Directive laying down basic safety standards for protection against the dangers arising from exposure to ionising radiation COM(2012) 242 final, 2011/0254 (NLE), 30 May 2012.
[63] EC Decision 2005/510/Euratom of 14 June 2005, Official Journal L185 (16 July 2005), pp. 33-40.

importance in the near future. Even without nuclear "renaissance", it will be a long term activity that goes beyond 2050. The Commission has indicated that currently 77 shutdown reactors are at various stages of decommissioning in the EU.[64] In addition, the decommissioning costs range between EUR 160 - 900 million per unit. One of the main problems, however, is the expected shortages of qualified nuclear staff needed in the decommissioning field. By 2020 some 40 000 new nuclear experts will be required, about 5 000 – 10 000 of them will have to acquire competence in the field of decommissioning and waste management.[65]

As it has been seen, following the Chernobyl reactor accident in 1986 the safety of Soviet-design reactors became a very sensitive issue, which was addressed in the last two EU enlargement processes. These accession discussions led to a decision for decommissioning of several reactors in the new Members States, in particular in Bohunice (Slovakia), Ignalina (Lithuania) and Kozloduy (Bulgaria). Accordingly, EU financial assistance programmes for Lithuania and Slovakia (2004) and for Bulgaria (2007) were established. The EU assistance scheme for decommissioning of nuclear power plants in those countries aims at reaching an irreversible state in the decommissioning process and eliminating the major source of radiological hazard. The total financial assistance to the three Member States until the end of 2013 foresees EUR 2 847.8 million in current prices (EUR 1 367 million for Lithuania, EUR 613 million for Slovakia and EUR 867.8

---

[64] See EC Presentation *"Overview of the European Nuclear Decommissioning Market"*, given at the European Forum for Science and Industry, Roundtable on *"Scientific Support for Nuclear Decommissioning"*, Brussels, 11 September 2012.
[65] *Ibid.*

million for Bulgaria).[66] The EU financial programmes to Lithuania and Slovakia provide the possibility of two alternative implementing channels: the first via the European Bank for Reconstruction and Development (EBRD), with contributions to the respective International Decommissioning Support Funds (IDSF), and the second via a national channel for a direct support through a National Agency.[67] For Bulgaria the EU assistance foresees the implementation only via the EBRD, given the absence of an appropriate national implementation structure.

The International Decommissioning Support Funds were established in 2000 and are managed by the EBRD. These funds are multidonor in nature, with the EU as the largest, and since 2004, the only contributor. For each of the three Member States a dedicated fund has been established: for Lithuania the Ignalina IDSF (IIDSF), for Slovakia the Bohunice IDSF (BIDSF) and for Bulgaria the Kozloduy IDSF (KIDSF).

Lastly, it is worth pointing out that in 2007, following the Council's conclusion on Commission's Communication "An Energy Policy for Europe"[68],[69] the European Nuclear Safety Regulators Group (ENSREG) was established to contribute to the

---

[66] EC Press Release "*Nuclear safety: EU will give extra EUR 500 million for the decommissioning of old Soviet type nuclear reactors*", IP/11/1449, 24 November 2011, available from: *http://europa.eu/rapid/press-release_IP-11-1449_en.htm#PR_metaPressRelease_bottom*

[67] Council Regulation 1605/2002 on the Financial Regulation applicable to the budget of the European Communities, Official Journal L 248, 16 September 2002, p.1.

[68] COM(2007) 1 final, Brussels, 10 January 2007.

[69] Presidency Conclusions, Brussels European Council (8-9 March 2007), Annex I, Chapter V, Paragraph 11, p. 23 - the Council endorsed the Commission proposal to set up an EU High Level Group on Nuclear Safety and Waste Management, available from *http://register.consilium.europa.eu/pdf/en/07/st07/st07224-re01.en07.pdf*

achievement of the Union's objectives in the field of nuclear safety.[70] As an independent authoritative expert body, ENSREG's role is to improve the overall transparency, cooperation and openness between the Member States on nuclear safety, radioactive waste and decommissioning issues. ENSREG also advises the Commission on additional European rules in the fields of the safety of nuclear installations and the safety of the management of spent, fuel and radioactive waste and it is obliged to submit a report to the EU institutions on its activities every three years.

---

[70] EC Decision of 17 July 2007 on establishing the European High Level Group on Nuclear Safety and Waste Management (which afterwards was renamed ENSREG), Official Journal L 195/44, 27 July 2007, pp. 44-46.

V. APPLICATION OF NUCLEAR SAFETY LAW BY THE MEMBER STATES

It can be said that nuclear safety law is a mixture of hard and soft law rules implemented by the Member States employing nuclear energy activities via three channels - the national statutory provisions; the Euratom and relevant EU Directives; and the International Atomic Energy Agency (IAEA) rules. The distinction between hard and soft law can be defined as a distinction between legally binding, enforceable provisions and general recommendations respectively. National legal hierarchies of nuclear safety law comprise several levels - constitutional level, statutory level (specific laws adopted by Parliaments), regulations (detailed rules adopted to control and regulate activities specified by statutory instruments) and non-mandatory guidance (proposed to clarify the legal requirements). All EU Member States that operate nuclear installations follow the basic principles set internationally for assuring nuclear safety and the safe management of radioactive waste and spent fuel. These principles are established in the Convention on Nuclear Safety[71] a nd the Joint Convention on the Safety of Spent Fuel Management and on the Safety of Radioactive Waste Management[72], promoted by IAEA. For example, the Conventions prohibit the operation of nuclear power plants without authorisation from the competent national regulatory body; an obligation which is reflected in the Member States' nuclear legal provisions.

---

[71] The Convention on Nuclear Safety, INFCIRC/449, IAEA, Vienna (1994)
[72] The Joint Convention on the Safety of Spent Fuel Management and on the Safety of Radioactive Waste Management, INFCIRC/546, IAEA, Vienna (1997)

It can be noted, that IAEA guidance documents and recommendations, such as the Safety Principles for Nuclear Power Plants and Safety Standards, are non-mandatory hierarchal set of documents, which plays an eminent role. These rules are the overarching set of soft law which is globally applicable within the field of nuclear safety. IAEA technical cooperation is an example of a good practice as IAEA technical guidance instruments have a direct impact at the national level in the Member States by ensuring the state of the art in nuclear technology. Whereas the international normative aspects of soft law have been greatly debated and appreciated, much implementation and research need to be done concerning the role of soft law within national jurisdictions. Although the technical norms, standards and guidelines in the field of nuclear safety, established by Member States' representative bodies, are also accepted in liability court proceedings as standard of due care (Germany, Belgium and UK), there are still outstanding issues, such as capacity building and technical cooperation, that should be aimed to be brought to a high level of harmonisation via inciting preliminary compliance with the soft law.

It is not always possible to detect the distinction between soft law and hard law. The application of nuclear safety law becomes more complex when legal instruments which are hard law in form, but soft law in content are examined. This is the case for the EU Directives mentioned in the previous chapter. Taking into account those EU provisions, two principles can be distinguished - justification and optimisation, which as such are hard law, but their application in the EU Member States is often without any guidance let alone effective control or sanctions.

In its Communication concerning the implementation of the Council Directive 96/29/Euratom the Commission stated that Article 6 of the Directive sets out the basic principle of radiation protection and thus requires the Member States to base their procedures on those principles, namely justification and dose limitation.[73] Hence, it can be concluded that the determination of the justification of any new type of practices, such as the radioactive protection, is the duty of each Member State. The justification principle has been applied accordingly in nuclear-safety proceedings in the United Kingdom where the Court stated that while the national statutory provisions (the Radioactive Substance Act of 1993) did not contain any requirements for justification, a Member State is obliged, to the extent possible, to apply its legislation in accordance with the relevant EU Directive.[74] As a result, it was decided that there was a legal obligation to justify any activity resulting in exposure to ionising radiation in conformity with Directive 96/29.

It should be noted, however, that the justification process involves complex issues of weighing up environmental discharges and impact, radiological effects, economics, safety and security and thus it may be a lengthy process and one which those

---

[73] Communication from the Commission concerning the implementation of Council Directive 96/29/Euratom of 13 May 1996, Official Journal C 133, 30 April 1998, p. 3.
[74] See *Friends of the Earth vs. The Secretary of State for Environment Food & Rural Affairs,* Court of Appeal of England and Wales, 7 December 2001, available from *http://www.ipsofactoj.com/international/2003/Part06/int2003(6)-014.htm*

opposing nuclear power plants will scrutinise heavily. Therefore, developers, regulators and governments should give due consideration as to how nuclear energy practices seeking justification are framed and then evaluated.

On the other hand, the optimisation principle (ALARA - As Low As Reasonably Achievable) takes into account social and economic factors. The demonstration of ALARA principle is carried out by implementation of regulatory guidance that indicates which numerical safety levels or safety objectives are mandatory and which are only guidance. ALARA is defined as a judgmental decision making process based on quantitative and qualitative approaches to select the appropriate protection solution.[75] For example, the application of ALARA principle for design purposes is achieved when national statutory provisions are introduced to ensure that potential radiation doses to the public and site personnel do not exceed prescribed limits and are as low as reasonably achievable.[76]

There are not many EU countries where a clear way of showing how ALARA principle should be applied can be seen. In the United Kingdom, the courts have determined that ALARA comprises two concepts - the standard of "duty of care" and "reasonable practicability". It is accepted that the test of reasonable practicability is an objective rather than subjective one, is

---

[75] See Steven Lierman and Ludo Veuchelen "*The Optimisation Approach of ALARA in Nuclear Practice: An Early Application of the Precautionary Principle? Scientific Uncertainty versus Legal Uncertainty*", European Environmental Law Review, April 2006, pp. 98-107.
[76] Western European Nuclear Regulators' Association (WENRA) "*Reactor Safety References Levels*", January 2007, p.9.

narrower than a "physically possible" test and that analysis is required between the quantum of risk and sacrifice involved taking into account the public perception and participation. This analysis includes "gross disproportionality test" execution showing a disproportion between the risk and the sacrifice, where the risk should be insignificant in relation to the sacrifice (whether in terms of money, time or trouble).[77] Therefore, the ALARA principle appears to be perceived as a risk management tool, which has been used by the courts to adjudicate the duty of care in situations where duty holders are required to identify and weigh up risks and possible control measures as well as to examine the precise nature of the relationship between them.

As it can be seen, nuclear safety law is largely created at international and European level, alongside principles and standards which in a number of cases find neither implementation nor control nor transparent enforcement mechanisms at national level. The overall picture of nuclear safety law in the EU consists of a mixture of hard and soft law, of command-and-control and performance-based regulations as well as of risk- and technology-based principles and standards. As a result, it is almost impossible for the national nuclear authorities to exercise proper management and control. Apart from the opposite positions of the Member States towards the use of nuclear energy, the reason for such an imbalance is the lack of clear distinction between hard and soft law provisions. Therefore, it is highly recommendable that the hierarchy between hard and

---

[77] Ludo Veuchelen "The Legal Value of General Principles, Technical Norms and Standards in European Nuclear Safety Law", European Environmental Law Review, August 2009, p. 223.

soft law be clearly spelled out as well as the hierarchy between different elements of the soft law be made reasonably explicit. Furthermore, soft law should be used as a benchmark for a general obligation in hard law so that the enforcement has practical strength.

VI. NUCLEAR RESEARCH

1. Euratom Seventh Framework Programme

The majority of nuclear research at European level is currently carried out under the Euratom Framework Programme for nuclear research and training activities. The main objective of this programme is to contribute to the exploitation of nuclear energy in a sustainable manner by making current technologies more economical and safer and by exploring new concepts. The Euratom programme is subdivided into two specific programmes - the first covers research into nuclear fusion (in particular ITER), nuclear fission and radiation protection whilst the second concerns activities by the Joint Research Centre (JRC) in the nuclear energy sphere, including nuclear waste management, nuclear safety, nuclear security and the environmental impact of nuclear energy. Since the Euratom Treaty limits all research programmes to a maximum of five years, initially the Euratom Seventh Framework Programme was adopted for the period 2007-11. Subsequently, it was extended with two more years (2012-13) in order to ensure the continuation of the EU funding in nuclear research activities and to bring the effective duration of the Euratom Framework Programme into line with the seven-year period of the main Seventh Framework Programme. The overall budget for implementing the Euratom Seventh Framework Programme amounts to EUR 5 251 million as a significant part of it is aimed to the fusion research - EUR 4 147 million, including the funding of the ITER. EUR 405 million is intended for nuclear fission and radiation protection whereas EUR 750 million is allocated to the nuclear activities of the JRC.[78]

1.1 Fusion technology

The largest share of EU nuclear research is carried out on fusion technology. Fusion technology is a process of fusing small atoms which releases substantial amounts of energy. In fusion reactions two light atomic nuclei fuse together to form a heavier nucleus (in contrast with fission power). In doing so, they release a comparatively large amount of energy arising from the binding energy due to the strong nuclear force which is manifested as an increase in temperature of the reactants. In the area of fusion energy, research is focused on developing the realisation of ITER and its operation.

ITER[79] (acronym of International Thermonuclear Experimental Reactor) is an international nuclear fusion research and engineering project, which is currently building the world's largest and most advanced experimental tokamak nuclear fusion reactor at the Cadarache facility in the south of France. It is

---

[78] Art. 3 of Council Decision of 18 December 2006 Concerning the Seventh Framework Programme of the European Atomic Energy Community (Euratom) for nuclear research and training activities (2007 to 2011) (2006/970/Euratom), Official Journal, 30 December 2006, p 66.

Art. 3 of Council Decision of 19 December 2011 Concerning the Seventh Framework Programme of the European Atomic Energy Community (Euratom) for nuclear research and training activities (2012 to 2013) (2012/93/Euratom), Official Journal, 18 February 2012, p 27.

The budget covers the whole period of seven years. The amount adopted for 2007-11 was EUR 2 751 million. Subsequently additional EUR 2 500 million was approved covering 2012-13 (Fusion Research: EUR 1 947 miilion + EUR 2 200 million; Fission research and radiation protection: EUR 287 million + EUR 118 million; JRC: EUR 517 million + EUR 233 million).

[79] The ITER Agreement was officially signed on 21 November 2006 in Paris. See *http://www.iter.org*

expected to demonstrate the scientific feasibility of fusion power, i.e. the physics required to achieve high power amplification that produces many times the amount of energy put into the experiment. The project is funded and run by seven members - the EU, India, Japan, China, Russia, South Korea and the United States. The EU, as host party for the ITER complex, is contributing 45% of the cost, with the other six parties contributing 9% each. The project is expected to cost more than EUR 10 billion over its 35-year lifetime to build, commission, operate and decommission. The construction of ITER began in 2007, and it is expected to be completed in 2020. The successful construction and operation of ITER will be a significant step towards the development of the first commercial demonstration fusion power plant (DEMO). Therefore, the information, technologies and experience provided by ITER will be crucial for bringing fusion energy to the commercial market. The DEMO is foreseen to start operation in the early 2040s whilst fusion is predicted to begin market penetration around 2050 with up to 30% of electricity production by 2100.[80]

---

[80] See *Fusion Electricity "A roadmap to the realisation of fusion energy"*, European Fusion Development Agency (EFDA - November 2012). The roadmap addresses three separate periods in the development of fusion energy with distinct main objectives:

1. Horizon 2020 (2014-2020) including five overarching goals - construction of ITER within scope, schedule and cost; securing the success of future ITER operation; preparation of ITER generation of scientists, engineers and operators; laying down the foundation of the fusion power plant DEMO; and promotion of innovation and industry competitiveness.

2. Second period (2021-2030) consisting of the exploitation of ITER up to its maximum performance and preparation of DEMO construction.

3. Third period (2031-2050) comprising the completion of ITER exploitation; as well as the construction and operation of DEMO.

It is worth mentioning that under the Euratom Seventh Framework Programme, not less than EUR 900 million of the whole fusion research budget (EUR 4 147 million) is reserved for activities other than the development of ITER.

1.2 Fission technology

Fission is the conventional nuclear technology that involves the splitting of large atoms into smaller nuclei. By carefully controlling this process at an industrial scale, large quantities of energy are released in order to generate electricity. The primary goal of fission research is to generate and exploit knowledge and develop scientific and technical competences and know-how in applied nuclear science and technology in the areas of safety, reliability, sustainability and cost-effectiveness of nuclear energy systems. The Euratom Seventh Framework Programme focuses on projects that address major issues and challenges in nuclear fission such as *ARCHER, FREYA, HARMONICS, PELGRIMM, SARGEN-IV* (nuclear installation safety); *ANDANTE, EpiRadBio, NERIS-TP, RENEB, SOLO* (radiation prection); *ALICE, EURACT-NMR, LACOMECO* (research infrastructure); *CORONA, EURECA!, TRASNUSAFE* (education and training) and most importantly *CATCLAY, IPPA, LUCOEX, PEBS, SKIN* in the field of management of radioactive waste.[81]

The management of radioactive waste has been a priority of the Euratom Framework Programme for many years. It focuses on two complementary management strategies: the first is the

---

[81] See EC, DG Research & Innovation *"Euratom FP7 Research & Training Projects"* (2012), Volume 3.

geological disposal of the most hazardous radioactive waste (essentially the most radioactive and radiotoxic forms of waste, which are either spent nuclear fuel or the vitrified residues from the reprocessing of this fuel to enable recycling of fissile material), and the second concerns the reduction of quantities and toxicity of waste material by chemical and nuclear processes.

1.3 Joint Research Centre (JRC)[82]

The nuclear activities of the Joint Research Centre focus on nuclear waste management, nuclear safety and nuclear security. In the area of radioactive waste and environmental impact, JRC aims to understand the nuclear fuel processes from production of energy to waste disposal and to develop effective solutions for the management of high level nuclear waste following two major options - direct disposal or partitioning and transmutation. In the field of nuclear safety, JRC implements research on existing and new fuel cycles and on reactor safety of both western and Russian reactor types as well as on new reactor design. It also conducts research and innovation activities in regard to the decommissioning of obsolete nuclear plants. In the nuclear security sphere, JRC supports the accomplishment of the EU's commitments, in particular the control of fuel cycle facilities, the monitoring of radioactivity in the environment, the implementation of additional protocol and integrated safeguards

---

[82] Joint Research Centre, located in Brussels, Belgium, is a Directorate-General of the European Commission (EC). JRC provides independent scientific and technical advice to the EC and Member States of the EU in support of EU policies. The EU through EC inherited JRC from Euratom. Originally JRC focussed on nuclear research, but its mission has been extended to fields like health and environment.

and the prevention of diversion of nuclear and radioactive material associated with illicit trafficking.

In addition JRC's activities include work carried out at the High Flux Reactor (HFR) in Petten (Netherlands), under a supplementary programme. HFR is owned by the Institute for Energy of the JRC. Its operation has been entrusted since 1962 to the Netherlands Nuclear Research and Consultancy Group (NRG). Since February 2005, NRG became also the license holder of the HFR. Together with the hot cells of NRG at the Petten site, the HFR has provided for over four decades integral and full complement of irradiation and post-irradiation examination services as required by current and future R&D for nuclear energy, industry and research organisations.

Furthermore, JRC manages and coordinates the European contribution to the Generation IV International Forum R&D initiative, in which the best research organisations in the world are involved.

3. Generation IV International Forum (GIF)

Generation IV International Forum is an international research project, which brings the world's leading nuclear technology nations together in order to develop a fourth generation of nuclear reactors.[83] GIF has thirteen Members which are signatories of its founding document, the GIF Charter. Argentina, Brazil, Canada, France, Japan, South Korea, South Africa, United

---

[83] See *http://www.gen-4.org/*

Kingdom and United States signed the GIF Charter in July 2001. Subsequently, it was signed by Switzerland in 2002, the Euratom Community in 2003, and more recently by China and Russia, both in 2006.

GIF is developing six nuclear energy systems that employ a variety of reactor, energy conversion and fuel cycle technologies. Their designs feature thermal and fast neutron spectra, closed and open fuel cycles and a wide range of reactor sizes from very small to very large. Depending on their respective degrees of technical maturity, the Generation IV systems are expected to become available for commercial introduction in the period between 2015 and 2030.

In regard to GIF, JRC acts as integrator of research with an aim of ensuring the quality of European contribution to the project. JRC contributes exclusively to those areas that can improve safety and safeguard aspects of innovative fuel cycles, in particular characterisation, test and analysis of new fuels, as well as to the development of safety and quality goals, safety requirements and advanced evaluation.

4. European Organisation for Nuclear Research (CERN)

The European Organisation for Nuclear Research, known as CERN[84], is an international organisation whose purpose is to operate the world's largest particle physics laboratory. Established in 1954, the organisation is based in the northwest suburbs of Geneva on

---

[84] CERN stands for Conseil Européen pour la Recherche Nucléaire.

the Franco–Swiss border. The term CERN is also used to refer to a laboratory, which employs just under 2 400 full-time employees, 1 500 part-time employees, and hosts some 10 000 visiting scientists and engineers, representing 608 universities and research facilities and 113 nationalities. CERN's main function is to provide particle accelerators and other infrastructure needed for high-energy physics research - as a result, numerous experiments have been carried out following international collaborations. In July 2012, researchers at CERN announced that they had observed a new particle, consistent with the long-sought Higgs boson.[85] The discovery is of significant importance since the new particle fits into place the last missing piece of a puzzle that physicists call the standard model of particle physics. This theory explains how particles interact via electromagnetic forces, weak nuclear forces and strong nuclear forces in order to make up matter in the universe.

Since its foundation by twelve Members in 1954, CERN regularly accepted new members. Generally, CERN's Members are also EU Member States, except Switzerland and Norway. Cyprus and Romania, as well as the non-EU countries Serbia and Israel, are Associate Members whereas Slovenia and the European Commission (as well as Turkey, Russia, UNIESCO, United States, India and Japan) have the status of Observer Members. However, Romania will become a full Member in 2015. CERN's budget for 2012 amounts to CHF 1 174.78 million.[86]

---

[85] CERN Press Release "CERN experiments observe particle consistent with long-sought Higgs boson" Press Office, 4 July 2012, available from
http://press.web.cern.ch/press-releases/2012/07/cern-experiments-observe-particle-consistent-long-sought-higgs-boson
[86] See CERN *"Final Budget of the Organization for the fifty-eighth financial year*

VII. FUTURE OF NUCLEAR ENERGY IN THE EU

As it has been seen, on the future of nuclear energy, the Member States can choose between several options – from the immediate ending of nuclear programmes to the construction of new plants, or even a gradual winding down which ensures a smooth transition to other energy forms. Given the major role of nuclear power in European energy production, any discussion of a reduction of its share in the energy mix makes it necessary to consider alternatives and replacement scenarios in the light of the three EU objectives that have to be achieved by 2020: a 20% reduction in greenhouse gas emissions relative to 1990 levels; a 20% share of electricity production to come from renewable sources; and a 20% reduction in energy consumption.[87] The decisions that have been taken in those crucial fields commit Member States and industries over decades and therefore require long-term planning.

In March 2011, the Commission proposed a "Road Map 2050"[88] as a long-term European strategy for this transition to a low-carbon economy. This communication proposes to stage ambitious and necessary climate objectives, with a reduction of green gas emissions 25% by 2020, 40%-60% by 2030-40 and

---

2012", 30 November 2011.

[87] These targets, known as the "20-20-20" targets, were set by EU leaders in March 2007, when they committed Europe to become a highly energy-efficient, low carbon economy, and were enacted through the climate and energy package in 2009.

[88] EC Communication "Energy Roadmap 2050", COM(2011) 885 final, Brussels, 15 February 2011. As an extension of the "Road Map 2050", the Commission expects to publish a specific road map for the energy sector, which details the options and various means of achieving the objective.

80%-95% by 2050, and envisages that energy production alone must support a reduction of 93-99% to become carbon-neutral. The Commission confirms that nuclear energy is a decarbonisation option providing today most of the low-carbon electricity consumed in the EU and as a large scale low-carbon option, it will remain in the EU power generation mix. It is also noted that nuclear energy contributes to lower system costs and electricity prices.

However, the Commission underlines the need for the highest safety and security standards to be further ensured by maintaining competence and technology leadership within the EU. In addition, safety costs and the costs for decommissioning existing plants and disposing of waste are likely to increase. At the European level, those waste and safety concerns will be addressed by developing new nuclear technologies (such as fourth generation reactors and fusion power) through the next Euratom Framework Programmes and the EU participation in the research projects discussed in the previous chapter. Furthermore, the Commission is committed to continue developing the nuclear safety and security framework and helping to set a level playing field for investments in Member States willing to keep the nuclear option in their energy mix.

The transition to a low-carbon society requires a diversification of the European energy mix, with both stimulation for clean, sustainable energy sources and research into new carbon-neutral technologies. In these circumstance, the role of each energy type (renewables, gas, coal, nuclear, etc.), their potential, advantages and disadvantages, will continue to be examined on the basis of rigorous and independent analyses. Although stakeholders, governments, energy producers, non-governmental organisations and other interest groups each argue for the promotion of one or another energy source to the detriment of others, it is expected that a large share of energy production in the future will come from renewables. Whereas the various fossil energy sources are most likely to play a complementary (transitional) role, the central issues lies in deciding what should be the share of nuclear energy.

Finally, it is worth mentioning that the difficult choice of an optimal energy source will be complicated by the continuing uncertainty over technologies which may affect the sustainability, competitiveness or safety of the respective source. This is the case for nuclear energy, as well as for other energy sources - gas (the potential of non-conventional sources such as shale gas), coal (CO2 capture and storage) and renewables (the potential of certain technologies to reduce development and production costs).

VIII. CONCLUSION

The debate over the future of nuclear energy must not be confined to experts, nor to politicians and business leaders. This is a crucial choice for the future of the European societies, and it calls for a public debate. The debate must be transparent and enlightened, and it must place in perspective the advantages and risks of nuclear energy in order for the public to make an informed opinion.

Nuclear energy in Europe has a transnational and even continental dimension. A major incident in a Member State's nuclear plant would inevitably have safety implications for neighbouring countries. Therefore, countries deciding to avoid nuclear power because of its risks would find themselves indirectly exposed by virtue of the sovereign choices made by a neighbouring Member States, and their safety would depend directly on the safety policy of that state. Moreover, the current integration of the EU's energy markets and networks is making the option of ending a nuclear programme somewhat artificial, since it will remain possible to import energy from nuclear sources in other countries.

For the reasons mentioned above, it would also be artificial to confine this debate to individual Member States. It is possible for the Member States to organise separate national debates which could take place in the same conditions and at the same time – as is already the case for the stress tests[89]. As an intermediate

---

[89] Following the nuclear accident in Fukushima, the Commission and the ENSREG

solution, there is also an opportunity for neighbouring Member States belonging to a shared region to organise collective debates. However, the EU faces complex and crucial choice to find an optimal energy solution in terms of sustainability, safety and competitiveness; it is therefore crucial for the discussion on the future of nuclear energy to take place at European level, in the framework of the emerging European energy policy and without excluding a revision of the Euratom Treaty.

---

agreed in May 2011 on voluntary tests for all operational nuclear power reactors in the EU. On 4 October 2012, the European Commission released the. Communication on the results of the stress tests (EC Communication on the comprehensive risk and safety assessments ("stress tests") of nuclear power plants in the European Union and related activities, COM(2012) 571 final). This document highlights that European nuclear power plants have generally high safety standards but further improvements are needed in almost all of them.

- THE END -

Bibliography:

EC Green Paper *"A European Strategy for Sustainable, Competitive and Secure Energy"* COM (2006) 105, 8 March 2006

EC *"EU Energy in Figures - Statistical pocketbook 2012"* (2012)

EC, DG Research and Innovation *"Euratom FP7 Research & Training Projects"* (2012), Vol. 3

EC, DG Research & Innovation *"Fission at glance"*

OECD Nuclear Energy Agency and International Energy Agency *"Projected costs of Generating Electricity"* (2010)

International Energy Agency *"World Energy Outlook 2012"*, published in November 2012

Massachusetts Institute of Technology *"Update of the MIT Future of Nuclear Energy - an Interdisciplinary MIT Study"* (2009)

Ross McCracken *"Nuclear Growth Faces Supply-side Constraints"* (2006), Energy Economist, Issue 297

The Economist *"Reacting Badly to Summer heat - Heavy Weather for Europe's Nuclear plants"* (2006), 10 August 2006

International Atomic Energy Agency *"Classification of Radioactive Waste"*, General Safety Guide, Vienna (2009)

EC *"Seventh Situation Report on Radioactive Waste and Spent Fuel Management in the European Union"* SEC (2011) 1007, 22 August 2011

EC, DG Research & Innovation *"Technology Platform for Implementing Geological Disposal launched"*, Press Release, 12 November 2009

Implementing Geological Disposal of Radioactive Waste Technology Platform *"Deployment Plan 2011–2016"* (2012)

Euratom Supply Agency *"Annual Report"* (2012)

"Europeans and Nuclear Safety" (2010), Special Eurobarometer 324 / Wave 72.2 – TNS Opinion & Social

Consolidated version of the Treaty establishing the European Atomic Energy Community, Official Journal C 84 of 30 March 2010

Thomas F. Gusack *"A Tale of Two Treaties: An Assessment of the Euratom Treaty in Relation to the EC Treaty"* (2003), Common Market Law Review, Vol. 40

Council Decision 2008/114/EC, Euratom of 12 February 2008 establishing Statutes for the Euratom Supply Agency, Official Journal L 41 of 15 February 2008.

Court of First Instance Judgement of 15 October 1995, cases T-458/93 and T-523/93, *ENU v. Commission*, ECR 1995, p. II 2459, point 67; Court of Justice Judgement of 11 March 1997, case C-337/95P, *ENU v. Commission*, ECR 1997

André Bouquet *"How Current are Euratom Provisions on Nuclear Supply and Ownership in View of the European Union's Enlargement?"* (2001), Nuclear Law Bulletin No. 68

Council Decision 77/270/Euratom of 29 March 1977, Official Journa L 88, 6 April 1977

EC, DG Economic and financial Affairs *"Ex-Post Evaluation of the Euratom Loan Facility*, 3 June 2011

Council decision 94/179/Euratom of 21 March 1994 amending Decision 77/270/Euratom, to authorise the Commission to contract Euratom borrowings in order to contribute to the financing required for improving the degree of efficiency and safety of nuclear power stations in certain non-member countries, Official Journal L84, 29 March 1994

Antony Froggatt "*The Extension of the Euratom Loan Ceiling: An Opportunity for Euratom Reform*", September 2002

EC "*White Paper: An Energy Policy for the European Union*" COM(95) 682, 13 December 1995

EC Communication "*Nuclear Industries in the European Union. An illustrative Programme According to Article 40 on the Euratom Treaty*", 25 September 1997, COM (97) 401

EC Communication "*Nuclear Illustrative Programme*" COM(2007) 565 final, 4 October 2007

Domenico Rossetti, Bruno Schmitz, Wiktor Raldow and Michel Poireu "*European Union Energy Research*" (2007) Revue de l'Energie, No 576, March - April 2007

EC Non-paper (29/09/2000)

Presidency Conclusions, Cologne European Council (3-4 June 1999)

Presidency Conclusions, Laeken European Council (14-15 December 2001)

EC Decision 1999/813/Euratom of 16 November 1999, Official Journal L318 (11.12.1999)

EC Communication "*Nuclear Safety in European Union*" COM (2002) 605 final, 6.11.2002

Case C-29/99, *Commission v. Council*, 10 December 2002, ECR I – 11221

Proposal for a Council Directive (EURATOM) setting out basic obligations and general principles on the safety of nuclear installations, COM (2003) 32 final, 30 January 2003

Council Directive 2009/71/Euratom of 25 June 2009 establishing a Community Framework for the nuclear safety of nuclear installations, Official Journal L 172/18, 2 July 2009

Council Decision of 14 December 1987 on Community arrangements for the early exchange of information in the event of a radiological emergency, Official Journal L 371, 30 December 1987

Council Resolution of 10 February 1980 on the implementation of a Community Plan of action in the field of radioactive waste, Official Journal C 051, 29 February 1980

Council Resolution of 15 June 1992 on the renewal of a Community Plan of action in the field of radioactive waste, Official Journal C 158, 25 June 1992

Proposal for a Council Directive (EURATOM) on the management of spent nuclear fuel and radioactive waste, COM (2003) 32 final, 30 January 2003

Council Directive 2011/70/Euratom of 19 July 2011 establishing a Community framework for the responsible and safe management of spent fuel and radioactive waste, Official Journal L 199, 02 August 2011

Council Regulation (Euratom) No 1493/93 of 8 June 1993 on shipments of radioactive substances between Member States, Official Journal L 148 , 19 June 1993

Council Directive 2006/117/Euratom of 20 November 2006 on the supervision and control of shipments of radioactive waste and spent fuel, Official Journal L 337, 05 December 2006

Directives of 2 February 1959 laying down the basic standards for the protection of the health of workers and the general public against the dangers arising from ionizing radiation, Official Journal No 11, 20 February 1959

Council Directive 96/29/Euratom of 13 May 1996 laying down basic safety standards for the protection of the health of workers and the general public against the dangers arising from ionizing radiation, Official Journal L 159 , 29 June 1996

EC Proposal for a Council Directive laying down basic safety standards for protection against the dangers arising from exposure to ionising radiation COM(2012) 242 final, 30.05.2012

EC Decision 2005/510/Euratom of 14 June 2005, Official Journal L185 (16 July 2005)

EC Presentation *"Overview of the European Nuclear Decommissioning Market"*, given at the European Forum for Science and Industry, Roundtable on *"Scientific Support for Nuclear Decommissioning"*, Brussels, 11 September 2012

EC Press Release *"Nuclear safety: EU will give extra EUR 500 million for the decommissioning of old Soviet type nuclear reactors"*, IP/11/1449, 24 November 2011

Council Regulation 1605/2002 on the Financial Regulation applicable to the budget of the European Communities, Official Journal L 248, 16 September 2002

EC Communication "An Energy Policy for Europe COM(2007) 1 final, Brussels, 10 January 2007

Presidency Conclusions, Brussels European Council (8-9 March 2007)

EC Decision of 17 July 2007 on establishing the European High Level Group on Nuclear Safety and Waste Management, Official Journal L 195/44, 27 July 2007

The Convention on Nuclear Safety, INFCIRC/449, IAEA, Vienna (1994)

The Joint Convention on the Safety of Spent Fuel Management and on the Safety of Radioactive Waste Management, INFCIRC/546, IAEA, Vienna (1997)

Communication from the Commission concerning the implementation of Council Directive 96/29/Euratom of 13 May 1996, Official Journal C 133, 30 April 1998

Friends of the Earth vs. The Secretary of State for Environment Food & Rural Affairs, Court of Appeal of England and Wales, 7 December 2001

See Steven Lierman and Ludo Veuchelen *"The Optimisation Approach of ALARA in Nuclear Practice: An Early Application of the Precautionary Principle? Scientific Uncertainty versus Legal Uncertainty"*, European Environmental Law Review, April 2006

Western European Nuclear Regulators' Association (WENRA) *"Reactor Safety References Levels"*, January 2007

Ludo Veuchelen *"The Legal Value of General Principles, Technical Norms and Standards in European Nuclear Safety Law"*, European Environmental Law Review, August 2009

Council Decision of 18 December 2006 Concerning the Seventh Framework Programme of the European Atomic Energy Community (Euratom) for nuclear research and training activities (2007 to 2011) (2006/970/Euratom), Official Journal, 30 December 2006

Council Decision of 19 December 2011 Concerning the Seventh Framework Programme of the European Atomic Energy Community (Euratom) for nuclear research and training activities (2012 to 2013) (2012/93/Euratom), Official Journal, 18 February 2012

Fusion Electricity "A roadmap to the realisation of fusion energy", European Fusion Development Agency (EFDA - November 2012)

http://www.iter.org

See *http://www.gen-4.org/*

CERN Press Release "CERN experiments observe particle consistent with long-sought Higgs boson" Press Office, 4 July 2012

CERN *"Final Budget of the Organization for the fifty-eighth financial year 2012"*, 30.11.2011

EC Communication "*Energy Roadmap 2050*", COM(2011) 885 final, Brussels, 15 February 2011

EC Communication on the comprehensive risk and safety assessments ("stress tests") of nuclear power plants in the European Union and related activities Brussels, 4 October 2012
COM(2012) 571 final